AMAZING
ANIMAL
ATLAS

HOW THE APP WORKS

This atlas includes a free app* that allows you to use your smartphone or tablet to get more information from each page. Follow the steps below to download and launch the app. You will discover 100 video clips and sounds from the world of nature.

*The **AmazingAnimalAtlas** app runs on iOS (11 or later) and Android (7 or later).
iOS: *iPhone* SE, 6s, 6s Plus, 7, 7 Plus, 8, X; all *iPad Pro* models and *iPad* (2017 onwards).
Android: you can find a complete list of compatible devices by scanning the QR code on the back of the cover or by visiting https://developers.google.com/ar/discover/supported-devices#google_play

1 DOWNLOAD THE APP

The app is available free of charge from App Store and Google Play. Type in "AmazingAnimalAtlas" and look for the icon shown here.
The information pages on each app store will tell you what operating system and device you will need to run the app. Click on the icon to download the app onto your smartphone or tablet.

2 LAUNCH AND SCAN

Launch the app. You will be asked to authorise access to your camera. The app works best in strong light and with flattened pages. Hover with your smartphone or tablet at least a foot above the pages (from 6 to 47). Large bouncy red dots will pop up on your screen.

3 WATCH, LISTEN, LEARN

Tap the red dots with your finger to trigger the videos. Sit back and enjoy the show!
This book has 100 videos.

First published in Great Britain in 2021
by NQ Publishers, an imprint of Nextquisite Ltd.

Copyright © 2017 by Nextquisite Ltd

www.nqpublishers.com
www.nextquisite.com

Project Director Anne McRae
Art Director Marco Nardi

Illustrations Alexander Vidal
Text Anne McRae
Editing Helen Woods
Picture Research Nicola Burns
Graphic Design Marco Nardi

ISBN 978-1-912944-73-6

Printed in China

Acknowledgments: National Geographic and Shutterstock for their video clips in the app

AMAZING
ANIMAL
ATLAS

Illustrated by Alexander Vidal

NQ
PUBLISHERS
For enquiring minds

TABLE OF CONTENTS

THE AMERICAS

THE FAR NORTH

AFRICA

EUROPE

AUSTRALIA AND THE PACIFIC

ASIA

THE SOUTH POLE

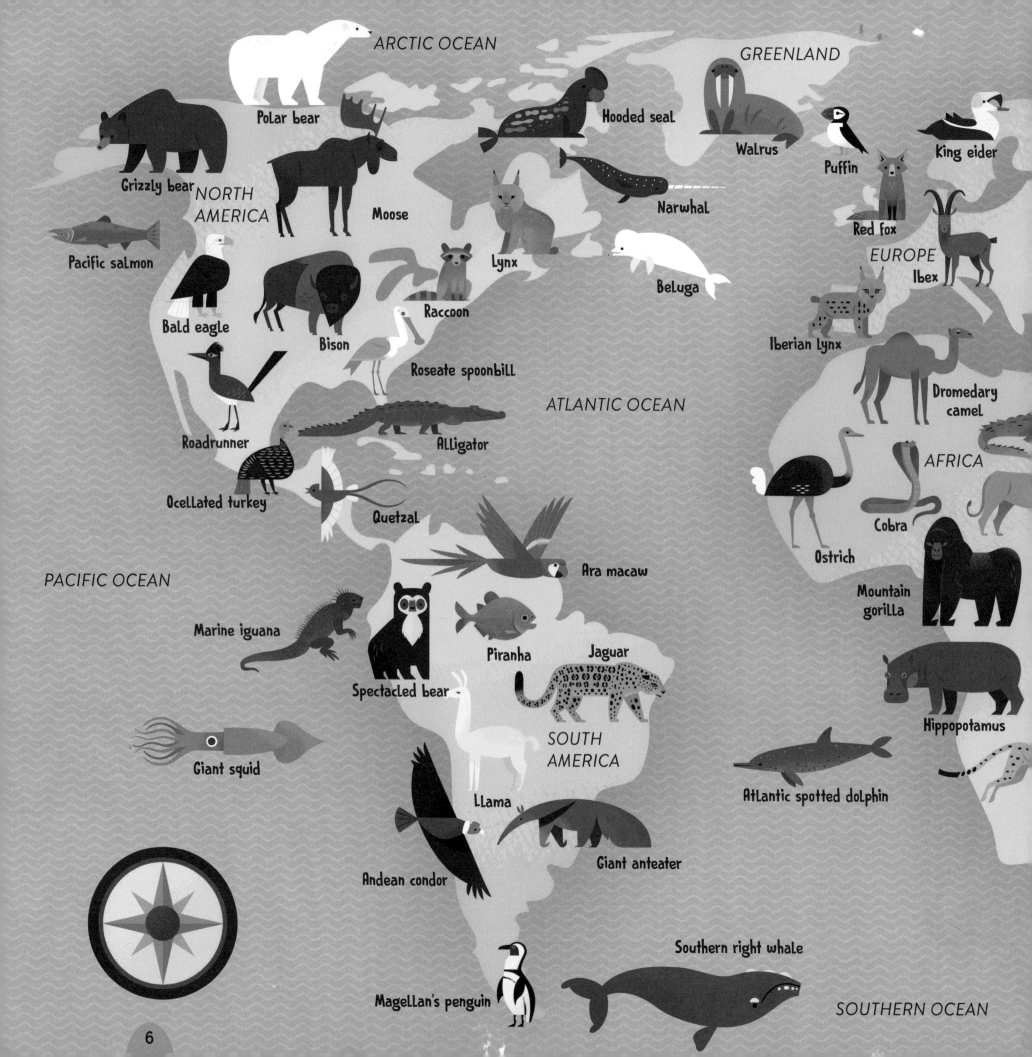

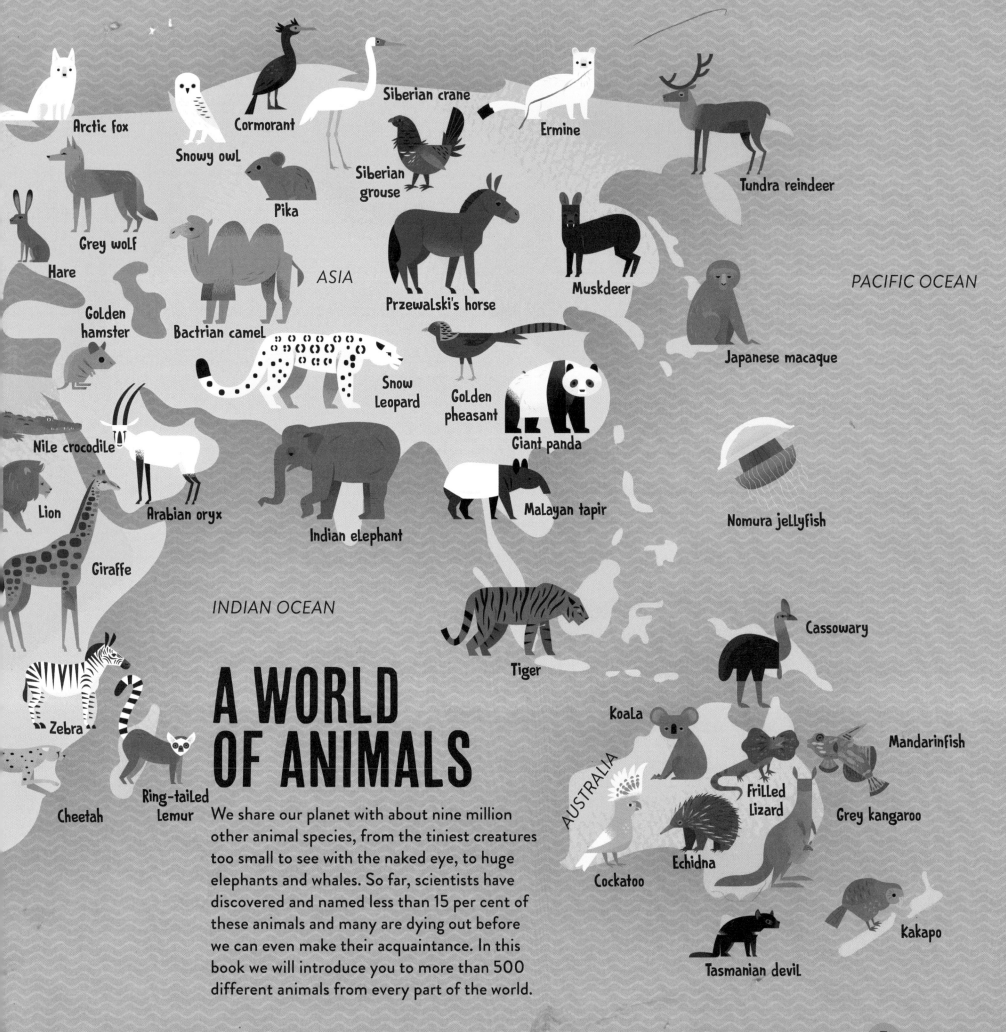

Arctic fox

Snowy owl

Cormorant

Siberian crane

Ermine

Tundra reindeer

Grey wolf

Pika

Siberian grouse

ASIA

Hare

Golden hamster

Bactrian camel

Przewalski's horse

Muskdeer

PACIFIC OCEAN

Japanese macaque

Nile crocodile

Snow Leopard

Golden pheasant

Giant panda

Lion

Arabian oryx

Indian elephant

Malayan tapir

Nomura jellyfish

Giraffe

INDIAN OCEAN

Tiger

Cassowary

Zebra

Koala

Mandarinfish

A WORLD OF ANIMALS

Cheetah

Ring-tailed Lemur

Frilled Lizard

Grey kangaroo

AUSTRALIA

We share our planet with about nine million other animal species, from the tiniest creatures too small to see with the naked eye, to huge elephants and whales. So far, scientists have discovered and named less than 15 per cent of these animals and many are dying out before we can even make their acquaintance. In this book we will introduce you to more than 500 different animals from every part of the world.

Cockatoo

Echidna

Kakapo

Tasmanian devil

THE ARCTIC AND GREENLAND

Only the hardiest animals can survive in the Arctic. In winter, temperatures can dip below −50°C (−58°F) and the sun is barely visible on the horizon, leaving the land in freezing twilight for months at a time. As the autumn days draw in, many animals head south to warmer places. But others stay put and thrive by changing their bodies or behaviour to cope with the cold. Some animals, like the polar bear, sleep through the winter, while others, such as the Arctic fox or snowy owl, turn white so they can blend into the white winter landscape and avoid being eaten by predators.

THE ARCTIC

The red dotted line on the map shows the Arctic Circle. Everything inside it is known as the Arctic.

Stoat

The stoat has a brown and white coat in the summer, but look at the ermine on the next page. Do you recognize it in its winter coat?

Lizard

Siberian newt

Caribou

Whiskered auklet

Pacific salmon (Chinook)

Salmon hatch from their eggs in rivers then they head out to sea for several years. When they are ready to breed they return upriver, often to the exact spot where they were born.

Ribbon seal

ALASKA

King crab

Many polar bears spend their lives floating on sea ice. As the Arctic ice cap melts because of global warming, their homes are disappearing and they are in danger of dying out.

Polar bear

Steller sea lion

Siberian crane

SIBERIA

Ermine

A stoat in its white winter coat is called an ermine.

King eider

Whooper swan

Greenland shark

SCANDINAVIA

Ptarmigan

Harp seal

Arctic octopus

Fulmer

THE NORTH POLE

There is no land under the North Pole, just permanently frozen sea.

Snow goose

Lumpfish

Red-faced cormorant

GREENLAND

Bowhead whale

Arctic fox

Arctic wolf

Walrus

Arctic tern

Wolf spider

Snowy owl

CANADA

Beluga

Greenland cod

Gyrfalcon

Pika

9

TUNDRA AND TAIGA

The treeless Arctic tundra stretches all the way around the top of the world. The stark landscape is frozen for most of the year and only low-growing plants like heather, mosses and lichen can survive. With icy temperatures, fierce winds and low rainfall, this is one of the harshest environments on the planet. Just below the tundra lies the world's largest forest—the taiga. Most of the trees are hardy conifers, such as pines, firs and spruces, and many animals make their homes here.

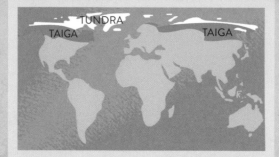

On this map the tundra is shown in white and the taiga in dark orange.

Snow sheep

Steller's sea eagle

Kronotsky volcano

Summer comes quickly on the tundra and lasts for just 50–60 days. Animals shed their winter coats and plants burst into flower while the sun shines overhead for 24 hours a day.

Kamchatka brown bears grow very large. They feast on berries, salmon and pine nuts, then sleep for six months through the winter.

Snowshoe hare

Kamchatka brown bear

Ptarmigan

Arctic bumblebee

Russian Arctic fox

Kamchatka swallowtail

Black-billed capercaillie

10

Wolverines eat animals and plants. They often travel more than 25 km (15 miles) a day in search of food.

Wolverine

Red crossbill

Moose

Siberian moth

Siberian tiger

Siberian tigers are the largest cats in the world. They live in the taiga where they have room to roam undisturbed.

Arctic ground squirrel

Squawk duck

Squawk ducks, also known as Baikal teals, breed in the tundra and taiga of eastern Russia. They fly south for the winter.

Salamander

NORTH AMERICA

North America is a vast place with every type of environment, from treeless tundra and tall mountains, to forests, prairies, lakes, rivers and deserts. Most of the best land has been taken for farming and many animals have been squeezed out of their homelands. There is still room for some wildlife, especially in remote areas of mountain and desert and in the far north. Some animals, such as bison and grey wolves, have been re-introduced in places where they once roamed freely and are now thriving again.

NORTH AMERICA

Fleet-footed pronghorns are among the fastest animals in North America. They have been clocked at 80 km (50 miles) per hour!

Pronghorn

More than 960 different species of mammal live in North America.

Grizzly bear

Awesome grizzly bears live by themselves most of the year, except for mothers and their cubs. But in the autumn the grizzlies gather together on riverbanks to catch salmon as they run upriver to spawn.

GREENLAND

Narwhal

Polar bear

Beluga

Caribou

Bighorn sheep

Walrus

Moose

ARCTIC OCEAN

Killer whale

Hooded seal

Lynx

Bald eagle

ATLANTIC OCEAN

Roadrunner

Speedy roadrunners live in the desert in the southern United States and Mexico.

Red fox

HUDSON BAY

Beaver

Canada goose

Raccoon

GREAT LAKES

Whooping crane

Virginia possum

Bison

Luna moth

Sage grouse

Roseate spoonbill

Alligator

Cougar

Porcupine

Skunk

Coyote

Ocellated turkey

Salmon (Sockeye)

Black-tailed jackrabbit

Gila monster

Rattlesnake

California sea lion

Axolotl

PACIFIC OCEAN

THE PRAIRIES

The vast grassy plains in the centre of North America are known as the prairies. The soil is rich and fertile and almost all the prairies have been turned into farmland. Agriculture has changed the environment, leaving it vulnerable to drought and erosion. Before the land was settled, millions of bison and other animals lived here. Now they are mostly restricted to national parks and reserves.

NORTH AMERICAN PRAIRIES

In spring, pronghorns gather in herds and migrate over long distances to summer pastures. They return to their winter lands in the autumn.

Pronghorn

Coyote

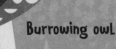

American badger

Burrowing owl

White-tailed jackrabbit

Black-footed ferrets

Black-footed ferrets were extinct in the wild until ecologists re-established them on the prairies.

Greater prairie chicken

Meadowlark

Monarch butterfly

Box turtle

Prairie falcon

Turkey buzzards

Bison

Bison are the largest land animals in North America.

Rainbow grasshopper

Prairie dogs live in huge burrows, called "towns," which they dig under the prairies.

Swift fox

Great Plains rat snake

Prairie dogs

CENTRAL AND SOUTH AMERICA

South America is dominated by the Andes, the longest mountain chain on the planet, and the Amazon jungle, the world's largest rainforest. But it also has vast grasslands, known as pampas and llanos, and the Earth's driest place — the Atacama Desert. These varied landscapes provide homes for a huge variety of animals, including many that are not found anywhere else. Only here will you find the world's largest rodent — the capybara — and its laziest animal — the sloth.

ATLANTIC OCEAN

CENTRAL AND SOUTH AMERICA

Most of Central and South America lie in the tropics.

CARIBBEAN SEA

Ara macaw

Ara macaws are large parrots with spectacular plumage.

Caribbean fruit bat

Blue tang

West Indian manatee

Quetzal

Three-toed sloth

Marine iguana

Darwin's finch

Galápagos penguin

GALÁPAGOS ISLANDS

Galápagos tortoise

Silky anteater

Toucan

Spectacled bear

Alpaca

Goliath bird-eating spider

Scarlet ibis

Piranha

Emerald tree boa

Jaguar

Tapir

Poison dart frog

Golden lion tamarin

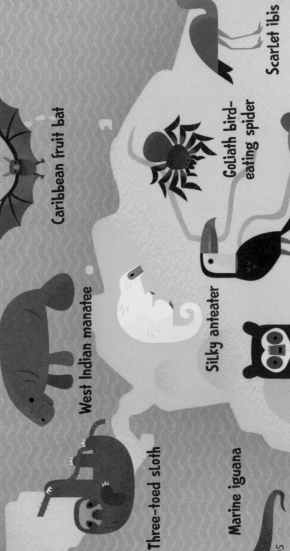

The Galápagos Islands lie almost 1,000 km (600 miles) off the coast of Ecuador. They are famous for the many unique animals that live there, and because it was here that Charles Darwin was able to verify many of his ideas about evolution.

Caiman

Capybara

Guanaco

Vicuña

Rhea

Southern right whale

Southern right whales live in the world's cool southern oceans. They have thick layers of blubber beneath their skins to protect them from the icy waters.

FALKLAND ISLANDS

Patagonian mara

Pink fairy armadillo

Magellan's penguin

Giant anteaters have long sticky tongues which they use to lap up more than 35,000 ants and termites every day.

Giant anteater

SOUTHERN OCEAN

Andean condor

PACIFIC OCEAN

Giant squid

Giant squid can grow to 13 metres (43 feet) long. They live far beneath the waves, in the ocean depths.

The llama and the alpaca are now domestic animals, but their close cousins the guanaco and the vicuña still live in the wild.

Llama

THE AMAZON

The Amazon is the largest rainforest in the world and it has more species of plants and animals than any other place on Earth. It lies in the Amazon river basin, an area about the size of the United States, and is criss-crossed by thousands of rivers. Here we can see the animals along a stream on the forest floor. Very little sunlight penetrates the thick vegetation of the canopy and it is gloomy and humid. The Amazon is not the only rainforest in Central and South America. There are many others, including some beautiful cloud forests which are wreathed in dense fog for most of the time.

CENTRAL AND SOUTH AMERICAN RAINFORESTS

Leafcutter ants

Harpy eagle

Blue morpho butterfly

Whistling duck

Tamandua

Tamanduas are a type of anteater. They live in the trees and feed mainly on ants and termites, but they also like bees and beetles.

Ocelot

Stealthy ocelots hunt for small mammals, birds and insects and fish at dusk and through the night.

Anaconda

Pink river dolphin

Pink river dolphins live in waterways throughout the Amazon jungle.

Electric eel

Coati

Two-toed sloth

Howler monkeys

Iguana

Hoatzins

Coypu

Giant river otter

Red-eyed tree frog

Highly intelligent and playful, giant river otters live together in family groups.

Assassin bug

More than half a million guanacos still roam free in the Andes.

THE ANDES

The Andes Mountains run right down the coast of South America, like a backbone for the continent. Many animals live in these towering, rugged mountains, some at very high altitudes. Animals that live high up have to cope with intense cold and air with less oxygen than at sea level. Many have thick coats and some have bigger lungs to breathe better, or special ways of circulating oxygen in their blood to give them the energy they need to survive in the thin air.

ANDES MOUNTAINS

The Andes are not a single line of mountains but a series of parallel peaks with high plateaus in between.

After it leaves the ground, the Andean condor rarely flaps its wings. It glides effortlessly among the mountain peaks on currents of air.

Guanacos

Hillstar

Andean mountain cat

Andean condor

The Andean flamingo is the rarest flamingo in the world. It lives in wetlands high up in the mountains.

Andean goose

Andean flamingo

Chinchilla

Titicaca grebe

Titicaca water frog

Cock of the rock

Yellow-tailed
woolly monkey

**Spectacled
bear**

Spectacled bears are the
only species of bear left in
South America. The others
are all extinct.

Mountain tapirs

Dyson's blue
doctor butterfly

Andean milk snake

Cougar

Pudu

Viscacha

AFRICA

Africa is home to many of our best-loved wild animals. Elephants, lions, zebras, cheetahs, giraffes, hippos and chimpanzees — to name just a few of the continent's famous creatures — all live here. More than anywhere else, animals are still able to live freely in the deserts, jungles and savannas that cover most of the land. However this is changing, and as more land is cleared for farming the animals have less space. They are also threatened by poachers who kill them for their skins or other body parts for fashion, ornaments and fake medicinal uses. Poachers also capture live animals for the illegal pet trade.

Lions live in family groups, called prides, which are made up of a dozen or more females, their cubs and two or three adult males.

Africa straddles the equator and has more tropical environments than any other continent.

EQUATOR

AFRICA

Lion

Mediterranean monk seal

MEDITERRANEAN SEA

Dromedary or one-humped camel

Scorpion

Egyptian cobra

Ostrich

Barbary sheep

Locust

Vulture

Grey parrot

Buffalo

Mountain gorilla

Pangolin

Okapi

Hyena

Nile crocodile

Jackal

Ethiopian wolf

Leopard

Picasso triggerfish

INDIAN OCEAN

Blue vanga

Ring-tailed Lemur

Elephant

African elephants are larger than their cousins in Asia, and their ears are shaped a bit like the continent of Africa (whereas Asian elephants have smaller, rounded ears).

Wildebeest

Gazelle

Warthog

Shoebill

Rhinoceros

Cheetah

Chimpanzee

Hippopotamus

Meerkat

Zebra

Manta ray

Atlantic spotted dolphin

ATLANTIC OCEAN

Giraffes are the tallest animals. They have long legs and very long necks that allow them to nibble on leaves much higher up on trees than any other animal can reach.

Giraffe

23

THE SAHARA

About the same size as the United States or China, the ever-expanding Sahara is the largest hot desert in the world. This is a place of extremes, where temperatures can sizzle above 45°C (110°F) in the summer and plunge below zero on winter nights. Rainfall is rare, although often torrential when it does come. Life is hard in the Sahara but many animals make their homes there.

SAHARA DESERT

The Sahara Desert covers most of North Africa.

Pin-tailed whydah

African silverbills

Sahara frog

Addax antelope

Saharan cheetah

Elegant addax antelopes change the colour of their coats with the season. They are white or blonde in the summer and brown and grey in the winter.

Fennec fox

Fennec foxes stay cool in burrows. At dusk they come out to forage for insects, eggs and rodents.

Dung beetle

Dung beetles roll dung into balls and bury them. They lay eggs in the dung and eat it!

Horned viper

Horned vipers ambush prey, paralysing them with their venom.

24

The Sahara rarely has clouds. The sun blazes from the blue sky almost every day of the year. At night, the sky is crystal clear.

Pharaoh eagle owl

Red-necked ostriches

Striped hyena

Anubis baboons

Slender-horned gazelle

Dromedary

Desert crocodile

This one-humped (dromedary) camel is cooling off in an oasis.

Nubian bustard

Egyptian cobra

An Egyptian cobra rears up ready to strike its prey.

Desert monitor

Gerbil

Gundi

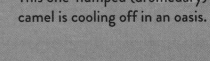

Deathstalker scorpion

Gerbils look like small kangaroos as they hop through the desert sands.

The deathstalker is the most lethal scorpion in the world.

Desert hedgehog

THE SAVANNA

Tropical grasslands, known as savannas, cover about half the land in Africa. These are vast areas of grass, low-growing bushes and a few scattered trees for shade. They are ideal for herbivores like antelopes, elephants, rhinoceros, gazelles and wildebeest. The predators that eat them, such as lions, jackals, vultures, leopards and hyenas, also thrive here.

AFRICAN SAVANNA

Hoopee

African wild dog

Oxpeckers

Some cheeky oxpeckers hitch a ride on the zebra.

Zebra

Impala

Southern ground hornbill

Lioness

A lioness and her cubs rest in the shade of an acacia tree.

Lion cubs

Cape porcupine

Aardvarks stay in burrows during the day. They come out at night to hunt for ants and termites which they dig out using their long sharp claws.

Aardvark

Black mamba

The deadly black mamba can kill with a single toxic bite.

Marabou

Mount Kilimanjaro

Elephants

Vervet monkey

Kudus are a type of antelope. There are more than 75 antelope species in Africa, from tiny dik-diks to giant elands.

Kudu

Giraffe

Lilac breasted roller

Termite mound

Chacma baboon

Banded mongoose

Cross section of a termite mound

Termites

Mound-building termites live in highly organized groups. The worker termites build large, complex mounds with tunnels and rooms and shafts for ventilation. Soldier ants guard the mounds.

Goliath beetle

27

EUROPE

Europe is densely populated and the land has been farmed intensively for centuries. There are very few wilderness areas left and many of the animals that remain have learned to live alongside humans. In the United Kingdom, foxes and badgers are now widespread in towns and cities, especially where the houses have gardens. These animals find that human refuse is a reliable source of food. In the countryside, many animals are making a comeback and there are now more bears, lynxes and wolves than there were 50 years ago.

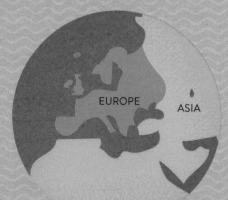

EUROPE ASIA

Puffin

Europe is joined to Asia and many of the same animals live in both continents.

ATLANTIC OCEAN

Harbour porpoise

At about 1.5 metres (5 ft) long, harbour porpoises are among the smallest marine mammals. They live in cool seas and like to stay close to shore.

Hedgehog

Red fox

Otter

Wild boars roam right across the Eurasian supercontinent, and they thrive in a variety of habitats, from deserts and mountains to woodlands and even big cities. Scientists have studied them in Berlin, where they make themselves at home in parks and gardens and feast on the rubbish.

The Barbary ape is the only wild monkey living on the European mainland. It stays on Gibraltar, on the southernmost tip of Spain.

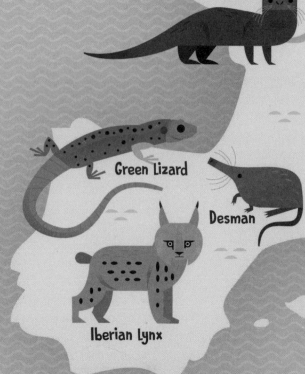

Green Lizard

Desman

Iberian Lynx

Atlantic cod

Elk

Arctic fox

Ural owl

Lemming

BALTIC SEA

Wolverine

Grey seal

NORTH SEA

Badger

Viper

Brown bear

Crow

Roe deer

Bison

Hare

Ibex

CASPIAN SEA

Giant mole rat

Stoat

Greek tortoise

BLACK SEA

Mute swan

Seahorse

Pine marten

Fire salamander

Peregrine falcon

Eagle owl

Swordfish

MEDITERRANEAN SEA

29

WOODLANDS

There are different types of woodland in Europe, from the evergreen conifer forests in the north to the deciduous woodlands in the centre. They all make ideal homes, providing food and shelter for a wide variety of animals. Bears, wild boars, beavers and deer are some common woodland mammals, but there are also snakes, frogs, insects and many birds too.

EUROPEAN WOODLANDS

Over one-third of Europe is still covered in trees, including managed forests.

Wild boar

Brown bears live all across Europe and Asia. This bear is enjoying a cooling dip in a woodland pond.

Brown bear

Wild boar piglets

Great spotted woodpecker

Goldfinch

Polecats are the wild ancestors of ferrets. They hunt and eat mice, rabbits, frogs and birds.

Polecat

Wildcat

Peacock butterfly

Mole

Edible dormouse

Edible dormice live in oak and beech forests. They feed on berries and nuts and hibernate for six months of the year. They were named by the ancient Romans, who loved to eat them!

Rabbit

Fallow deer

Bluetit

Grey heron

A tall grey heron wades through the pond searching for insects and fish to gobble up.

Beavers were hunted almost to extinction in Europe. They have been re-introduced in many areas and are thriving there.

Beaver

Grass snakes usually live close to water. They are not venomous but prey on frogs and toads, as well as birds and fish. They sleep though the winter. The females lay 30–40 leathery eggs in early summer.

Toad

Stag beetle

Grass snake with eggs

THE MEDITERRANEAN

Life on land can be tough in the Mediterranean region, where the long summers are hot and dry and the winters short and wet. In many ways life in the water is easier and with about 15,000 different animal species living there, the Mediterranean Sea is a hotspot for marine life.

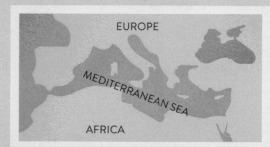

The Mediterranean is the sea that lies between Africa and Europe. The region around the sea is also known as the Mediterranean.

Striped dolphin

Striped dolphins live in pods of 25–100 animals. They "talk" using clicks and whistles.

Devil fish

Despite its name, the devil fish is a shy creature that dives deep into the ocean. It also likes to leap right out of the sea!

Sperm whale

Sperm whales have the largest brain of any animal. Like most sea mammals, they use clicks and other sounds to communicate and to find things using a process called echolocation.

The shortfin mako can go at 35 km/h (22 mph), making it the fastest shark in the world. It also makes spectacular leaps up to six metres (20 feet) out of the water.

Shortfin mako shark

Parrotfish

Zebra sea bream

Spider crab

Conger eel

Sea gulls breed in large colonies along the Mediterranean coast.

Yellow-Legged gull

Spanish imperial eagle

Greater flamingo

Flamingos wade in the shallow lagoons and lakes, turning their heads upside down beneath the waves as they filter food through their beaks.

Squid

Loggerhead turtle

White-spotted octopus

Red sea stars

Scorpionfish

Spiny Lobster

Mussels

33

ASIA

Asia stretches almost halfway round the globe and has every kind of environment, from chilly taiga and steppe to hot deserts and rainforests. There are more animals here than on any other continent. But there are also more people, and many animals are being pushed to extinction by human activity. Conservationists are working hard to stop this, with mixed results. Successes include the giant panda which was taken off the WWF's Endangered List in 2016.

Asia is the biggest continent. It covers almost a third of the Earth's land.

Tigers are the largest of the big cats and adult males can weigh up to 300 kg (660 lb). They once ranged across Asia, but are now restricted to just a few areas where they are threatened by loss of habitat and hunting.

ASIA

Grey wolf

Baikal seal

Sable

Bactrian camel

Saiga

Sand cat

Dhole

Yak

Golden hamster

Onager

Caracal

Indian cobra

Indian rhinoceros

Arabian oryx

Indian elephant

Tiger

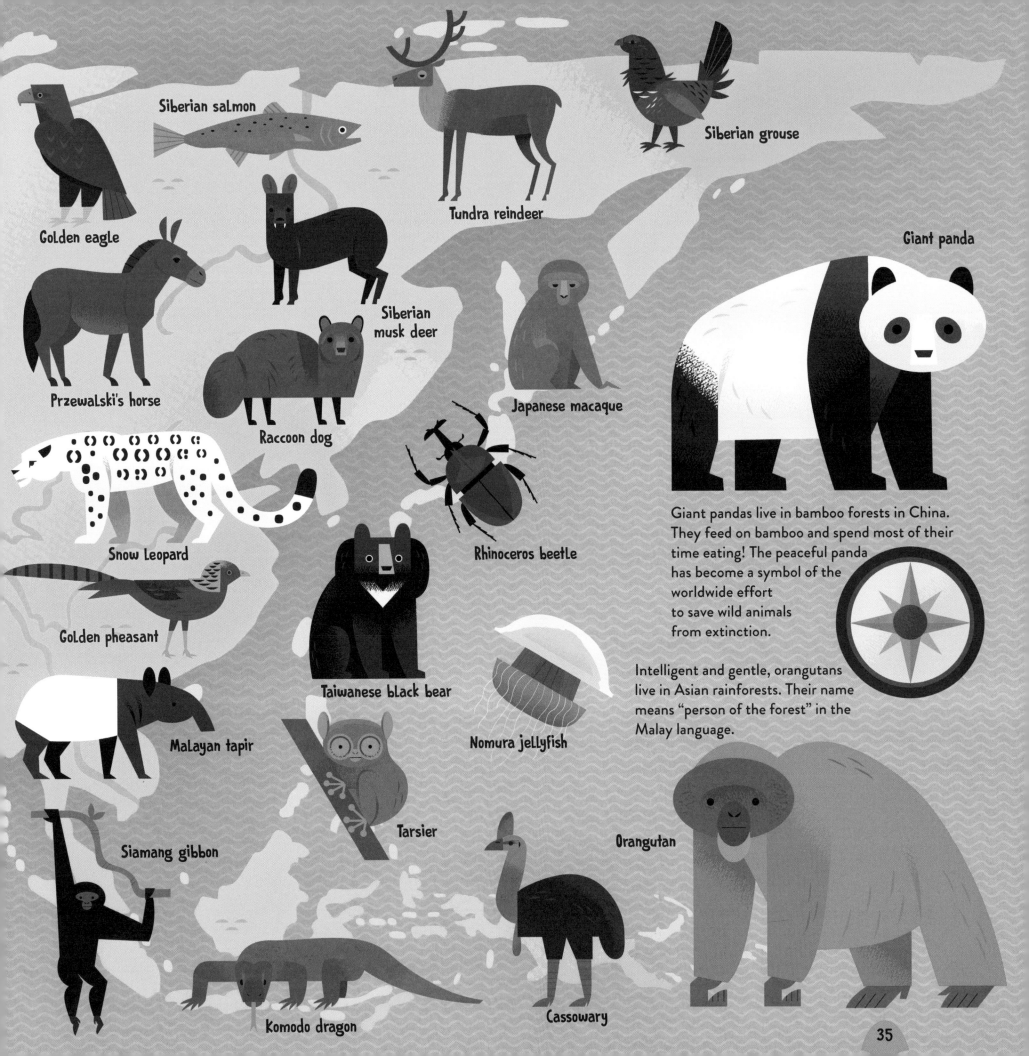

Golden eagle

Siberian salmon

Tundra reindeer

Siberian grouse

Giant panda

Przewalski's horse

Siberian musk deer

Raccoon dog

Japanese macaque

Rhinoceros beetle

Snow Leopard

Golden pheasant

Taiwanese black bear

Giant pandas live in bamboo forests in China. They feed on bamboo and spend most of their time eating! The peaceful panda has become a symbol of the worldwide effort to save wild animals from extinction.

Malayan tapir

Nomura jellyfish

Intelligent and gentle, orangutans live in Asian rainforests. Their name means "person of the forest" in the Malay language.

Tarsier

Siamang gibbon

Orangutan

Komodo dragon

Cassowary

THE STEPPE

The Eurasian steppe was the original home of the horse and this is where people first tamed horses and learned to ride them. The steppe is home to many large grazing animals, such as sheep and antelopes, but also to lots of burrowing rodents and keen-eyed birds.

EUROPE   THE STEPPE

ASIA

The steppe is a vast belt of grasslands that runs all the way across Asia and into eastern Europe.

Steppe wolf

The steppe wolf, also known as the Caspian sea wolf, lives in small packs. The females give birth to four to seven pups which are raised by all members of the group.

Turkestan Lynx

Black-tailed gazelle

Saiga

Black stork

Lapwing

The saiga has an inflatable hump on its nose which it uses to filter out dust in the summer and to heat the icy air in winter.

Black vulture

Steppe fox

Steppe marmot

Argali are the world's largest wild sheep. They are hunted for their horns, which are used in Chinese medicine, and are now an endangered species.

Argali sheep

The Tolai hare rests in a hollow in the ground during the day. It comes out at dusk to nibble on grasses, herbs and roots.

Tolai hare

Pallas' cat

Steppe eagle

Stone marten

Steppe tortoise

Pallas' cats have strange flat heads and a lot of thick, fluffy fur. When excited, Pallas' cats yelp and growl more like a small dog than a cat.

Pit vipers have large venomous fangs and can open their mouths very wide to bite and swallow prey.

Long-eared hedgehog

Central Asian pit viper

37

ASIAN RAINFORESTS

About ten per cent of the world's tropical jungles are in Southeast Asia. These are the oldest rainforests on Earth. They have existed for at least 70 million years but now logging, mining, farming and poaching are gradually destroying them and the animals that have always lived there.

Asian rainforests are now mainly restricted to Southeast Asia.

SOUTHEAST ASIA

Sun bears are the smallest species of bear and they are rare and shy. They are hunted for their fur and have been pushed from their jungle homes.

Sun bear

Great hornbill

Flat-headed cat

Skywalker gibbon

The skywalker gibbon was named as a new species in 2017. The scientists who named it are big fans of Star Wars!

Masked palm civet

Java leaf insect

Flying foxes

Loris

Red-breasted parakeet

Reticulated
python

Reticulated pythons are the longest
snakes in the world, and among the
heaviest. They ambush prey and squeeze
it to death in their long body coils.

Baby
orangutan

Rajah Brook birdwing butterfly

Oriental dwarf
kingfisher

Proboscis
monkey

Binturongs, also
known as bearcats,
spend a lot of time in
the trees where they
feast on fruit.

The secretive Sunda clouded leopard lives
alone in the jungles of Sumatra and Borneo.

Sunda clouded
leopard

Binturong

39

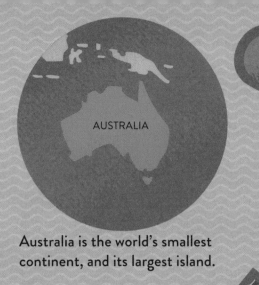

AUSTRALIA

Koala

Australia is the world's smallest continent, and its largest island.

AUSTRALIA

Australia has more unique animals than any other continent. It broke away from the rest of the land on our planet millions of years ago and the animals living there have evolved in special ways. Today you can find amazing marsupials, like kangaroos and numbats, and egg-laying mammals such as echidnas, that don't exist anywhere else. Australia also has a lot of really scary animals whose bite or sting could knock you right out.

Koalas live in eucalyptus trees and feast on the leaves.

INDIAN OCEAN

The saltwater crocodile, or "saltie", can grow up to seven metres (23 feet) long. It is the largest reptile in the world, and one of the most dangerous.

Reticulated swellshark

Snubnose dolphin

Blue-tongued skink

Kookaburra

King brown snake

Red kangaroo

Thorny dragon

Mallee fowl

Cockatoo

Emu

Short-beaked echidna

Numbat

Saltwater crocodile

Leafy sea dragon

Little penguin

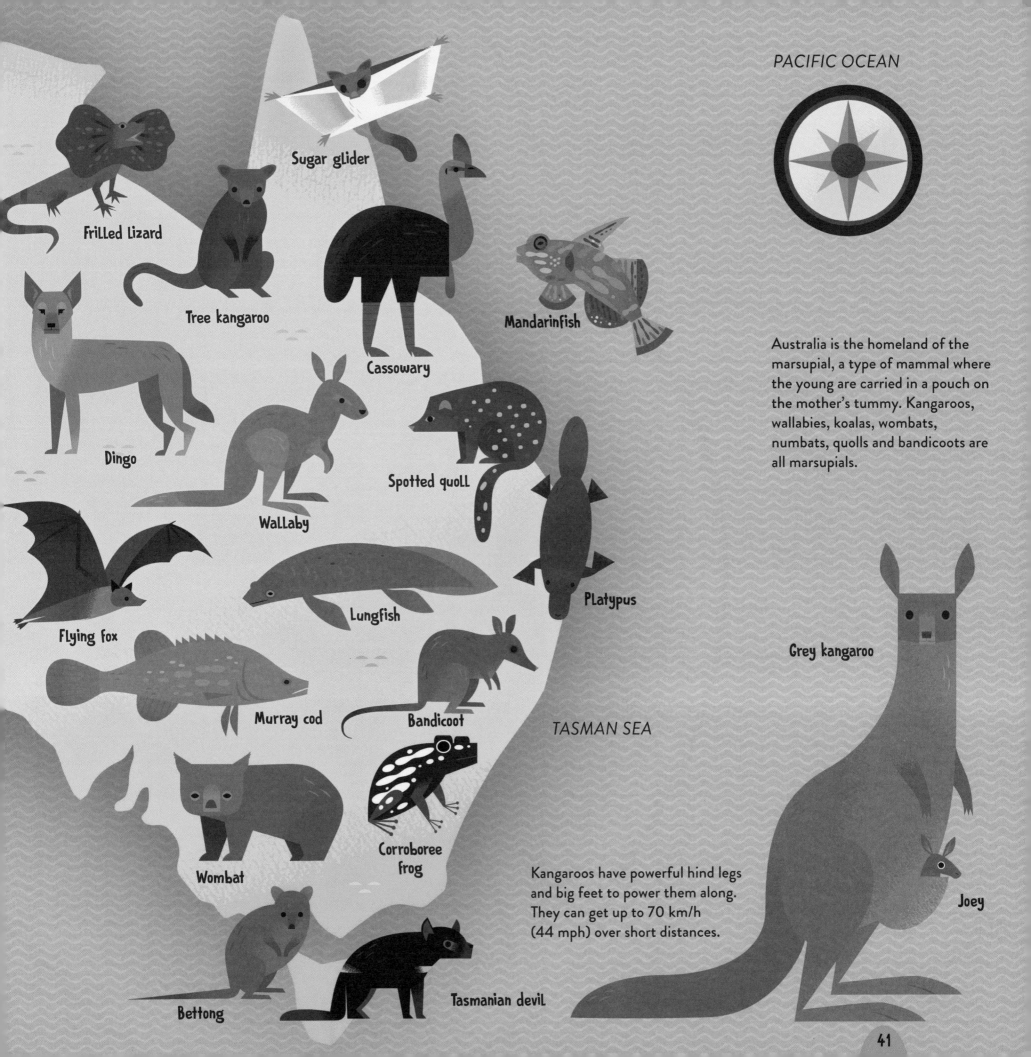

PACIFIC OCEAN

Sugar glider

Frilled lizard

Tree kangaroo

Cassowary

Mandarinfish

Dingo

Wallaby

Spotted quoll

Flying fox

Lungfish

Platypus

Murray cod

Bandicoot

TASMAN SEA

Wombat

Corroboree
frog

Bettong

Tasmanian devil

Grey kangaroo

Joey

Australia is the homeland of the marsupial, a type of mammal where the young are carried in a pouch on the mother's tummy. Kangaroos, wallabies, koalas, wombats, numbats, quolls and bandicoots are all marsupials.

Kangaroos have powerful hind legs and big feet to power them along. They can get up to 70 km/h (44 mph) over short distances.

41

THE GREAT BARRIER REEF

The largest coral reef in the world lies off the coast of Australia. Known as the Great Barrier Reef, it is made up of 3,000 individual reefs and 900 tiny islands. It is 2,300 km (1,400 miles) long and is home to more than 1,500 species of fish. The reef is a UNESCO World Heritage site but is threatened by pollution and global warming.

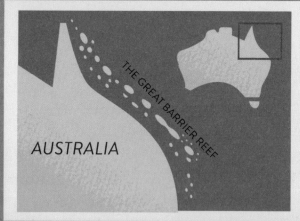

AUSTRALIA

THE GREAT BARRIER REEF

The Great Barrier Reef is the world's largest living structure and is visible from outer space.

The Great Barrier Reef was formed 6,000 to 8,000 years ago.

Cardinal fish

Angelfish

Butterfly fish

Surgeonfish

Tomato grouper

Harlequin tuskfish

Hammerhead shark

Spotted eagle ray

Damselfish

Parrotfish

Triggerfish

Sunset wrasse

Sea anemone

Clownfish

Tube sponge

Humpback whale

Whale-watching boat

Humpback whales live in seas and oceans all over the world. Male humpbacks sing complex "songs" that can last 10–20 minutes.

Humpback dolphin

Painted sweetlips

Sea turtle

Scientists fear that the Great Barrier Reef is dying, along with many other coral reefs around the world. Most of the damage is caused by global warming as sea temperatures rise above what the corals can withstand.

Coral trout

Coral

Diver

Napoleon wrasse

TENTACLE   MOUTH

Coral reefs are made up of millions of tiny stony corals. When they die, the stony corals' hard skeletons remain and after many decades, or centuries, a coral reef is gradually formed.

STOMACH

Potato cod

Cross section of a stony coral

White-tipped reef shark

Giant clam

Gobies

Flying fox

Guam rail

Hawaiian monk seal

NORTH PACIFIC OCEAN

Coconut crab

Great frigatebird

PAPUA-NEW GUINEA

SOLOMON ISLANDS

Dugong

VANUATU

White-spotted surgeon fish

AUSTRALIA

Yellow-bibbed Lory

NEW CALEDONIA

FIJI

Coconut octopus

Many-coloured fruit dove

New Zealand sea Lion

Tuatara

Fiji banded iguana

Mudskipper

Kakapo

NEW ZEALAND

Weta

Tawaki (Fiordland crested penguin)

New Zealand is home to more flightless birds than any other place in the world. There are 16 flightless species there, and 16 more species that have gone extinct.

Masked angelfish

Pulelehua

Grey whale

Pacific bluefin tuna

Pacific sailfish

Mahimahi

Ultramarine Lorikeet

Black sea turtle

Red-tailed tropic bird

TAHITI

EASTER ISLAND

COOK ISLANDS

Mangaia kingfisher

Flat-tailed sea snake

THE PACIFIC OCEAN

PACIFIC OCEAN

SOUTH PACIFIC OCEAN

Frilled shark

Some strange creatures live in the ocean depths, like this frilled shark, which has physical features that were common in the time of the dinosaurs. Scientists call it "a living fossil".

The Pacific Ocean covers about one-third of the surface of the planet. It is so big that it could hold all the planet's landmasses, and still have room left over.

The Pacific is the largest and deepest ocean in the world. There are more than 25,000 Pacific islands, including coral reefs. Scientists can only guess at how many animals live here because so many species have yet to be discovered or named. In recent years, researchers have put electronic tags on animals such as sharks, whales, birds, seals and even squid, so that they can track their movements and learn about how they live.

ANTARCTICA

This is the coldest, windiest and most remote place on Earth. Almost all the land is covered in a sheet of ice at least a mile thick. Very little rain falls so, despite the ice and snow, Antarctica is a desert. Just a few animals live here all year round and most stick to the coast where the sea makes it slightly warmer. The majestic Emperor penguin is the only animal that breeds here in the winter. The Emperors march inland in the autumn to form large nesting colonies.

Antarctic petrel

Emperor penguins

Minke whale

Antarctic petrel

Crabeater seal

Emperors are the largest of all penguins. They huddle together in groups on the ice to stay warm.

Emperor penguin chicks

Despite their name, these seals don't eat crabs. They fill up on krill.

Imperial shag

Adelie penguins

Adelie penguins live all around the coast of Antarctica. They spend the winter on pack ice at sea because it is warmer.

46

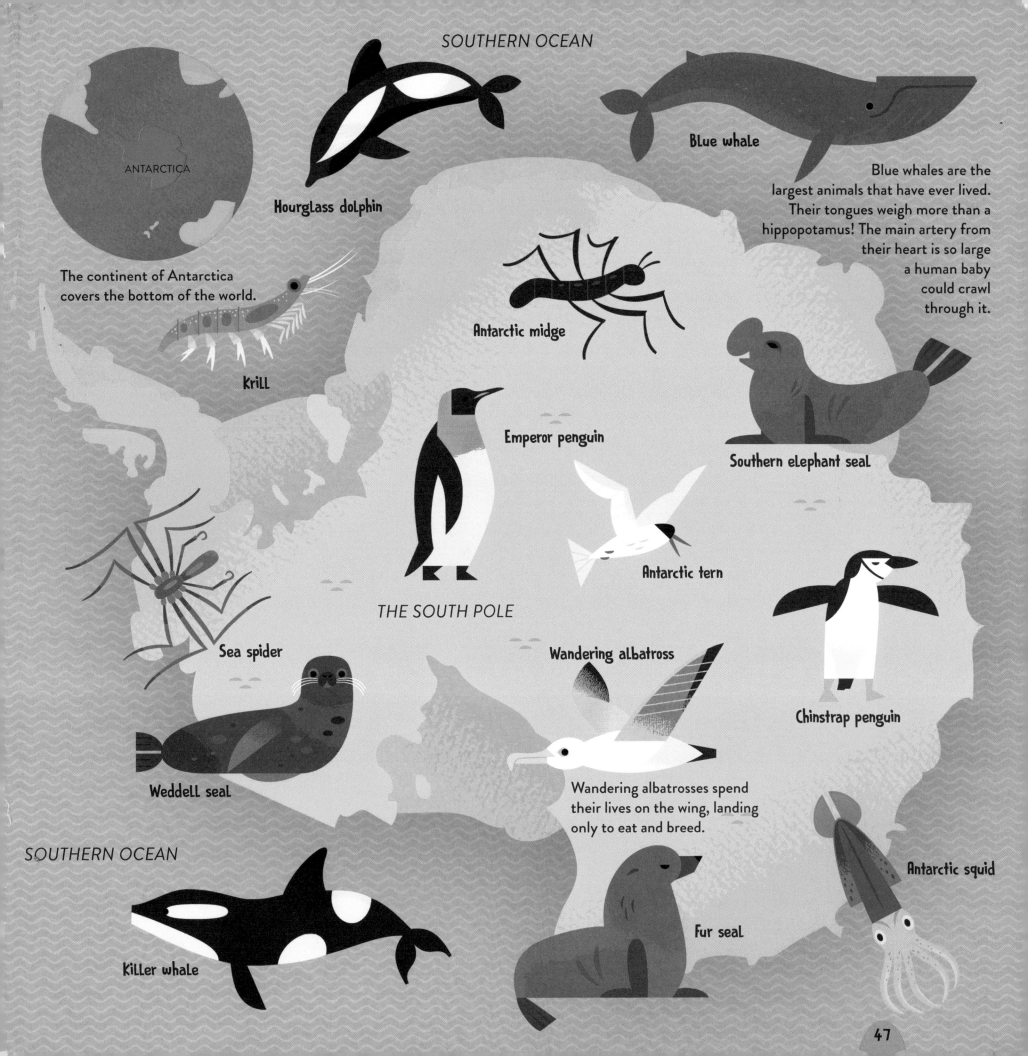

ANTARCTICA

The continent of Antarctica covers the bottom of the world.

Hourglass dolphin

Krill

Antarctic midge

Blue whale

Blue whales are the largest animals that have ever lived. Their tongues weigh more than a hippopotamus! The main artery from their heart is so large a human baby could crawl through it.

Southern elephant seal

Emperor penguin

Antarctic tern

THE SOUTH POLE

Sea spider

Wandering albatross

Chinstrap penguin

Weddell seal

Wandering albatrosses spend their lives on the wing, landing only to eat and breed.

Antarctic squid

Killer whale

Fur seal

INDEX